GW01237722

More Pencil Fun 1

S. Cassin & D. Smith

Illustrated by A. Rodger

Collins: Glasgow and London

© 1981 C.E.M.A.
0 00 197030 5
This impression 1986
Printed in Great Britain

Circles

A page to practise the anti-clockwise movement.

1 Talk about the page, making anti-clockwise movements with your finger round the circular objects.

2 Find a 5p coin and place it on the second sun. Starting at the heavy dot, draw round the coin.

3 Repeat with all the objects, starting at the heavy dot each time. Colour the page.

Further activities: Draw round more coins on a piece of paper, always using an anti-clockwise movement. Colour them alternately red and blue.

ore practice in the anti-clockwise movement.

Talk about the page, making anti-clockwise movements with your finger round the circular objects.

Find a 5p coin and place it on the second face. Starting at the heavy dot, draw round the coin.

Repeat with all the objects, starting at the heavy dot each time. Colour the page.

urther activities: Find different sized circles to draw round, remembering always to start at '1 o'clock'.

c and o

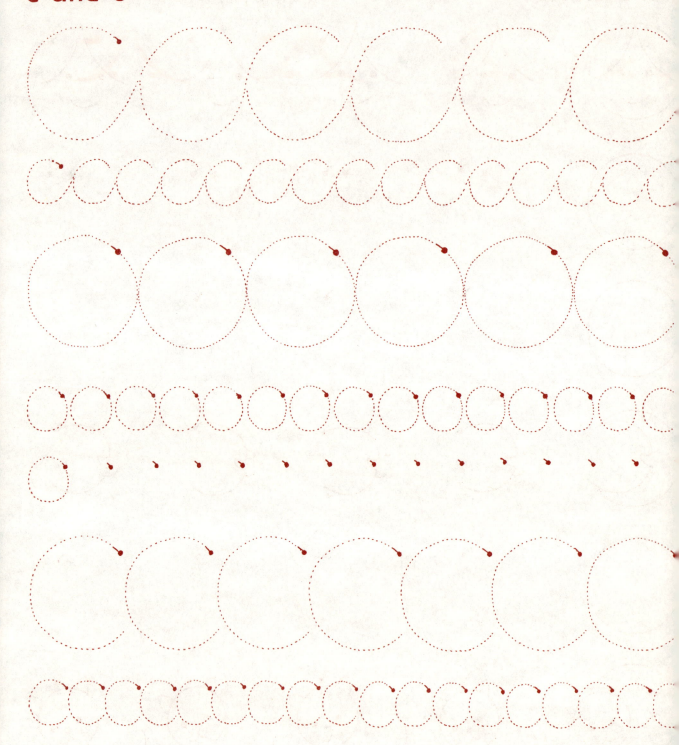

A page to practise **c** and **o**.

1 Talk about the page and remind your child of the anti-clockwise movement.

2 Complete the first two lines by following the dots from left to right, first with a finger, then with pencil, using one continuous movement for each pattern.

3 Complete the letters, remembering to start at the heavy dot.

Further activities: Find pictures of objects beginning with either **c** or **o**. Write the appropriate letter big and bold on each picture.

page to practise **e**.

Talk about the page.

Complete the pictures and letters by following the dotted lines, first with a finger, then with pencil. Remember to start at the heavy dot.

Practise the letter **e** in the blank spaces, and colour the page.

Further activities: Find pictures of words beginning with **e** and write a big **e** on each one.

Round and round

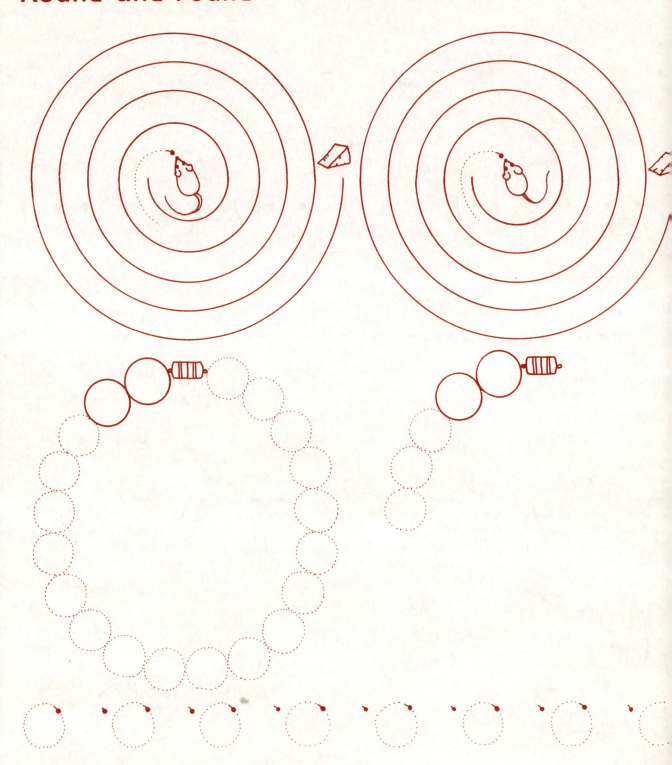

More anti-clockwise practice.

1 Talk about the page. Practise the anti-clockwise movement in the air.

2 Point with your finger, moving in an anti-clockwise direction, to show how the mouse escapes, then complete the lines with crayon.

3 Complete the beads on the necklaces, remembering to start at '1 o'clock' each time.

4 Practise the letter **o** in the blank spaces, and colour the page.

a and d

A page to practise **a** and **d**.

1 Talk about the page and practise the anti-clockwise movement in the air.

2 Complete the pictures and letters by following the dotted lines, first with a finger, then with pencil. Remember to start at the heavy dot.

3 Practise the letters in the blank spaces, and colour the page.

q and g

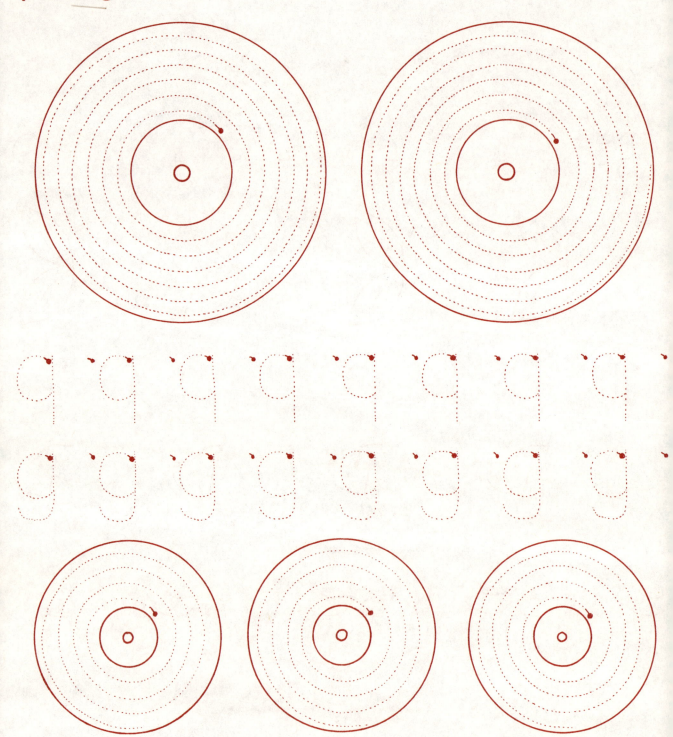

A page to practise **q** and **g**.

1 Talk about the page and practise the anti-clockwise movement in the air.

2 Point with your finger to show how the record groove runs, then complete the lines with crayon.

3 Complete the letters by following the dotted lines, first with a finger, then with pencil. Remember to start at the heavy dot.

4 Practise the letters in the blank spaces, and colour the page.

A page to practise **s**.

1 Talk about the page, and the correct place to start the letter **s**.

2 Complete the pictures and letters by following the dotted lines, first with a finger, then with pencil.

3 Practise **s** at the foot of the page, without using any guidelines.

First words

A page to practise the letters covered so far.

1 Talk about the page and name the objects illustrated.

2 Taking one word at a time, discuss where each letter starts. Trace the letters, first with a finger, then with pencil or felt pen.

3 Write each word again in the boxes provided, read it, and colour the picture.

and j

A page to practise **i** and **j**.

1 Talk about the page and practise drawing lines in the air. Always start at the top.

2 Complete the pictures and letters by following the dotted lines, first with a finger, then with pencil. Remember to start at the heavy dot.

3 Practise the letter **j** in the blank spaces, and colour the page.

Straight lines

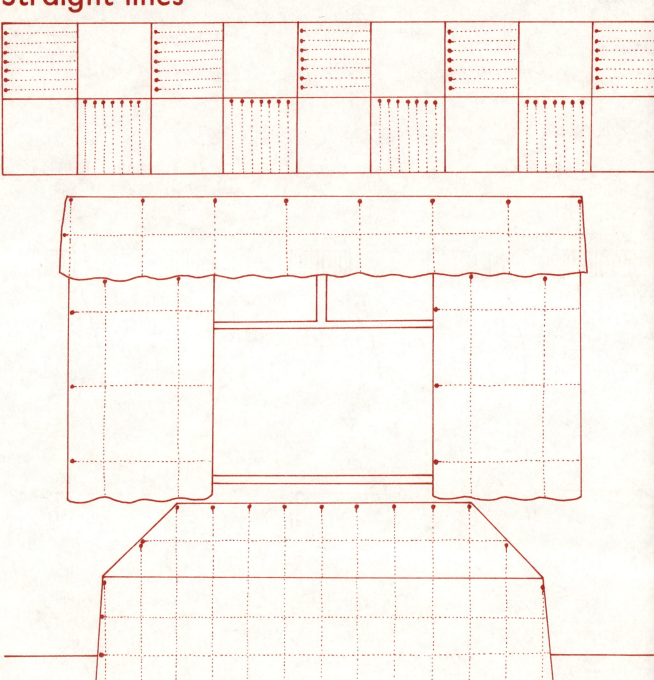

Practice in horizontal and vertical lines.

1 Talk about the page and practise drawing lines in the air. Always start at the top, or at the left-hand side.

2 Complete the lines and pictures by following the dotted lines, first with a finger, then with pencil. Remember to start at the heavy dot.

Further activities: Draw and colour patterns using horizontal and vertical lines.

A page to practise **f** and **j**.

1 Talk about the page. Practise ∫ and ⌡ in the air, starting at the top.

2 Complete the pictures and letters by following the dotted lines, first with a finger, then with pencil. Remember to start at the heavy dot.

3 Colour the page.

Further activities: Find pictures of objects beginning with either **f** or **j**. Write the appropriate letter big and bold on each picture.

More words

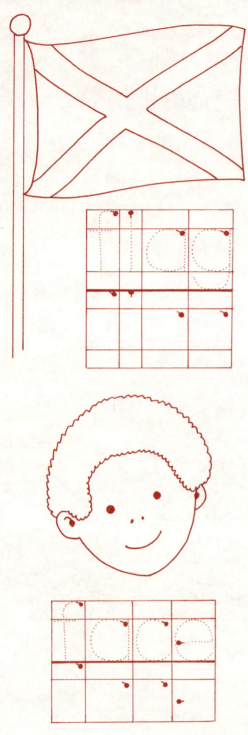

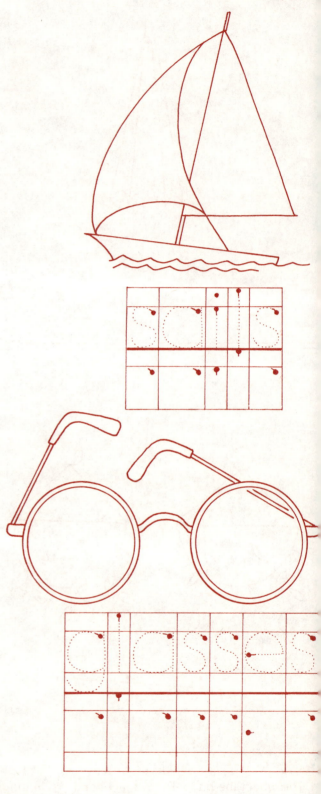

A page to practise the letters covered so far.

1 Talk about the page and name the objects illustrated.

2 Taking one word at a time, discuss where each letter starts. Trace the letters, first with a finger, then with pencil or felt pen.

3 Write each word again in the boxes provided, read it, and colour the picture.

Further activities: Find other words using some of these letters, and write them.

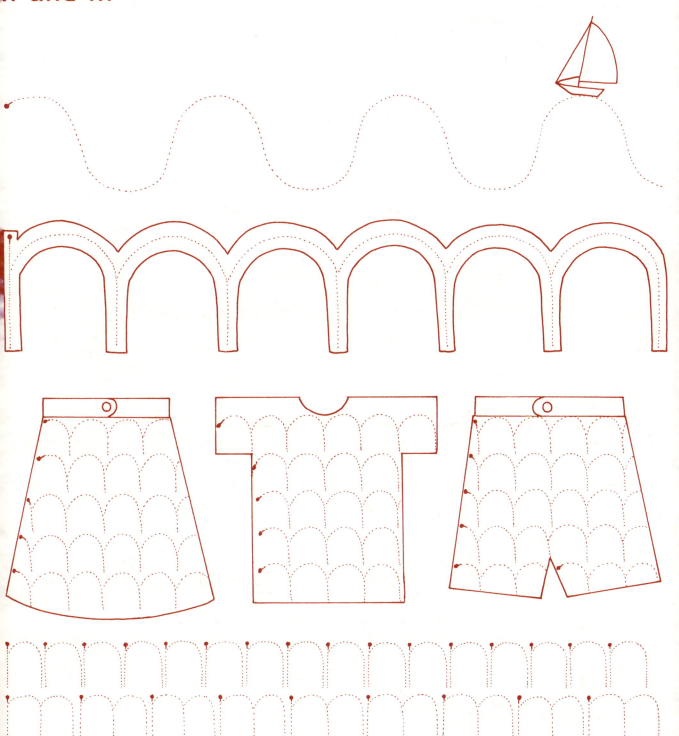

Patterns using **n** and **m**.

1 Talk about the page. Draw m and wavy lines in the air with a finger, using one continuous movement.

2 Complete the patterns by following the dotted lines, first with a finger, then with pencil. Remember to start at the heavy dot.

3 Colour the page.

Further activities: Paint a picture of boats and waves. First paint the waves, then the boats.

r and h

A page to practise **r** and **h**.

1 Talk about the page. Remind your child of the wave pattern and practise it in the air.

2 Complete the pictures and letters by following the dotted lines, first with a finger, then with pencil. Remember to start at the heavy dot.

3 Practise the letters in the blank spaces, and colour the page.

Further activities: Use crayons or felt pens on a large piece of paper to make big flowers using the pattern practised above.

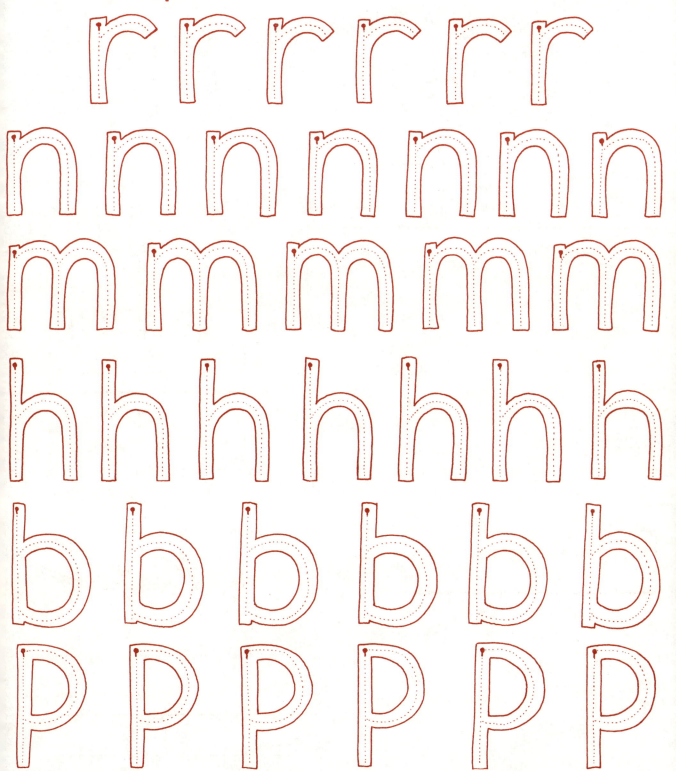

A page to do more work on **r**, **n**, **m**, **h**, **b** and **p**.

1 Talk about the page and discuss where each letter starts.

2 Trace the letters by following the dotted lines, first with a finger, then with pencil.

3 Colour the page.

Words again

hedgehog

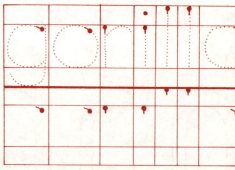

gorilla

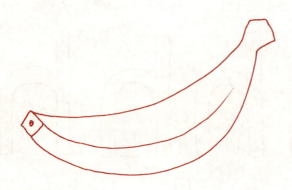

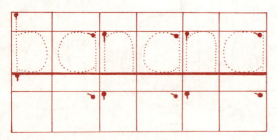

banana

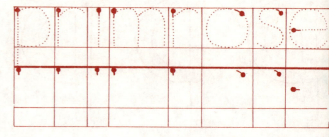

primrose

A page to practise the letters covered so far.

1 Talk about the page and name the objects illustrated.

2 Taking one word at a time, discuss where each letter starts. Trace the letters, first with a finger, then with pencil or felt pen.

3 Write each word again in the boxes provided, read it, and colour the picture.

More straight lines

Another page to practise straight lines.

1 Talk about the page and identify the objects illustrated.

2 Complete the pictures by drawing over the dotted lines.

3 Colour the pictures.

Further activities: Draw large squares on a sheet of paper and ask your child to make pictures using a ruler.

Christmas

More lines to draw and pictures to make.

1 Talk about the page and identify the objects illustrated.

2 Complete the pictures by drawing over the dotted lines.

3 Colour the pictures.

A page to make your own picture.

1 Talk about the page and identify the objects illustrated.

2 Complete the pictures by drawing over the dotted lines.

3 Colour the page to make an attractive scene.

Further activities: Draw and paint your own pictures using these shapes.

A windmill

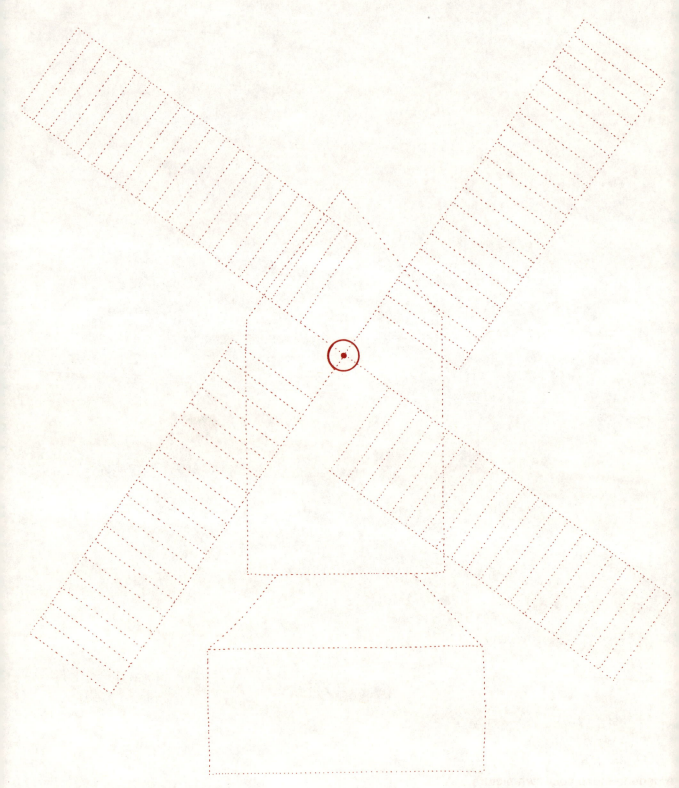

Another page to practise straight lines.

1 Talk about the page.

2 Complete the windmill by drawing over the dotted lines.

3 Colour the picture.

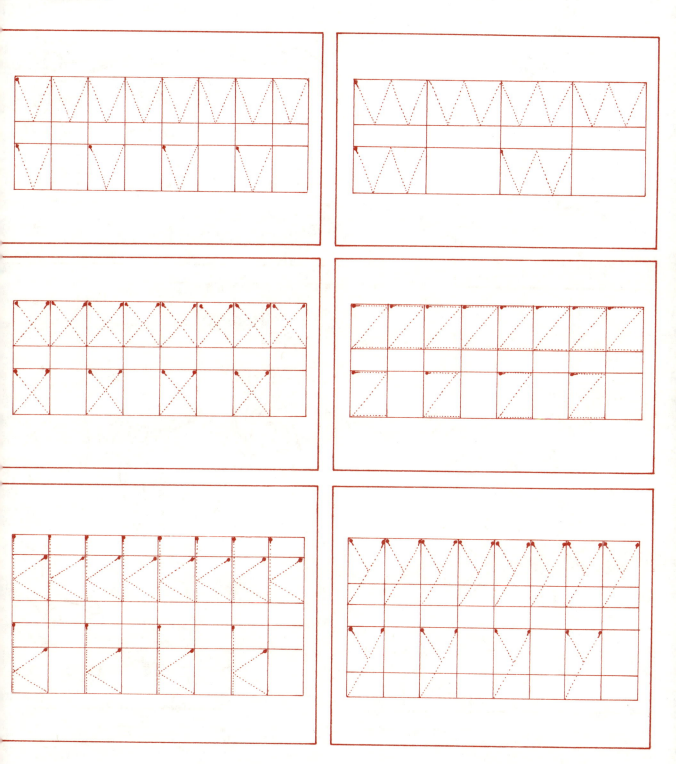

Making patterns with **v, w, x, z, k** and **y**.

Talk about the page. Discuss where each letter starts.

Trace the letters by following the dotted lines, first with a finger, then with pencil. Remember to start at the heavy dot.

Practise the letters in the blank spaces, and colour the page.

Even more words

A page to practise some of the letters covered so far.

1 Talk about the page and name the objects illustrated.

2 Taking one word at a time, discuss where each letter starts. Trace the letters, first with a finger, then with pencil or felt pen.

3 Write each word again in the boxes provided, read it, and colour the picture.

A page of **u** and **t** patterns.

Talk about the page.

2 Complete the patterns by following the dotted lines, first with a finger, then with pencil. Remember to start at the heavy dot.

3 Colour the page.

Further activities: Use a mixture of thick paint and paste to cover a big sheet of paper. Then practise this pattern with your index finger in the wet paint.

More and more words

A page to practise some of the letters covered so far.

1 Talk about the page and name the objects illustrated.

2 Taking one word at a time, discuss where each letter starts. Trace the letters, first with a finger, then with pencil or felt pen.

3 Write each word again in the boxes provided, read it, and colour the picture.

Dutch girl and boy

A page to practise manual control.

1 Talk about the page.

2 Complete the pictures by tracing over the dotted lines, first with a finger, then with pencil or crayon.

3 Colour the page.

Further activities: Draw a large person on a sheet of paper and use patterns like these to fill in the clothes.

Fish

More practice in manual control.

1 Talk about the page.

2 Complete the fish by tracing over the dotted lines, first with a finger, then with pencil or crayon.

3 Colour the page.

Further activities: Cut some fish shapes out of newspaper and use felt pens to make patterns on them. Stick them onto some blue paper.

I can write words

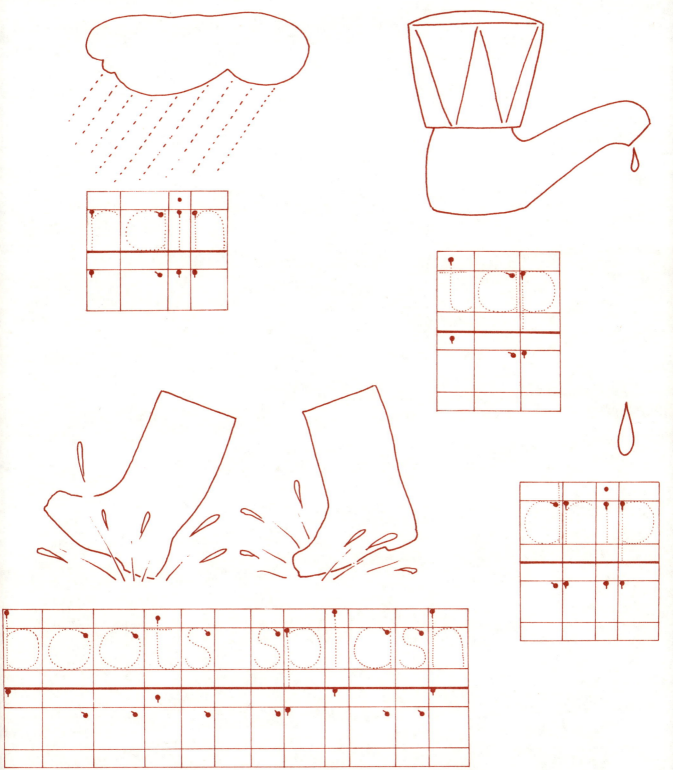

More letter practice.

1 Talk about the page and name the objects illustrated.

2 Taking one word at a time, discuss where each letter starts. Trace the letters, first with a finger, then with pencil or felt pen.

3 Write each word again in the boxes provided, read it, and colour the picture.

More patterns

A page to practise the manual control needed to write numerals.

1 Talk about the page.

2 Complete the patterns by following the dotted lines, first with a finger, then with pencil or felt pen.

3 Colour the page.

Further activities: Make more patterns using paint and a brush.

Numbers

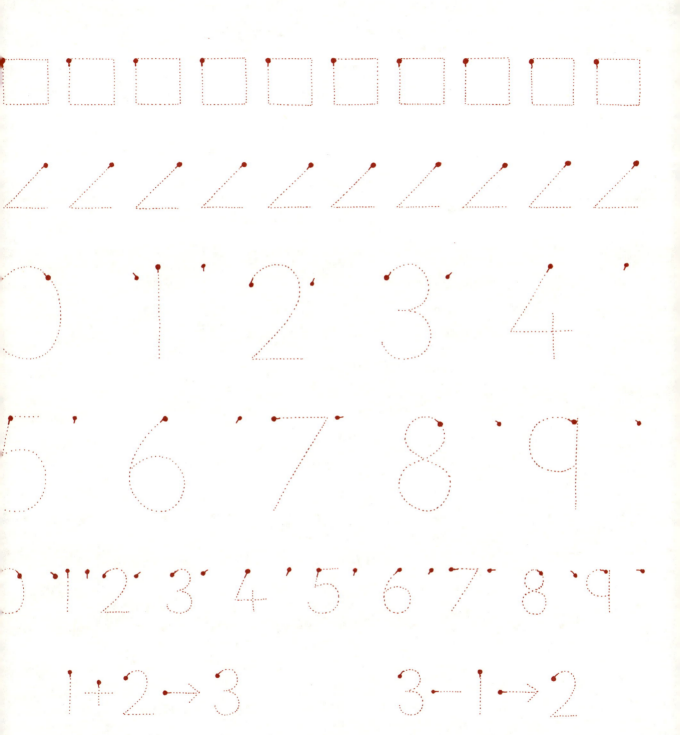

page to practise writing numbers.

Talk about the page and discuss where each number starts.

Complete the shapes and numbers by following the dotted lines, first with a finger, then with pencil or felt pen.

Colour the page.

Further activities: Paint the numerals 0 to 9 on a large sheet of paper.

About me

my name is

I am a

I am   years old.

I go to school.

I read and write.